Hello.
My name is Anxiety.

I live inside your head.

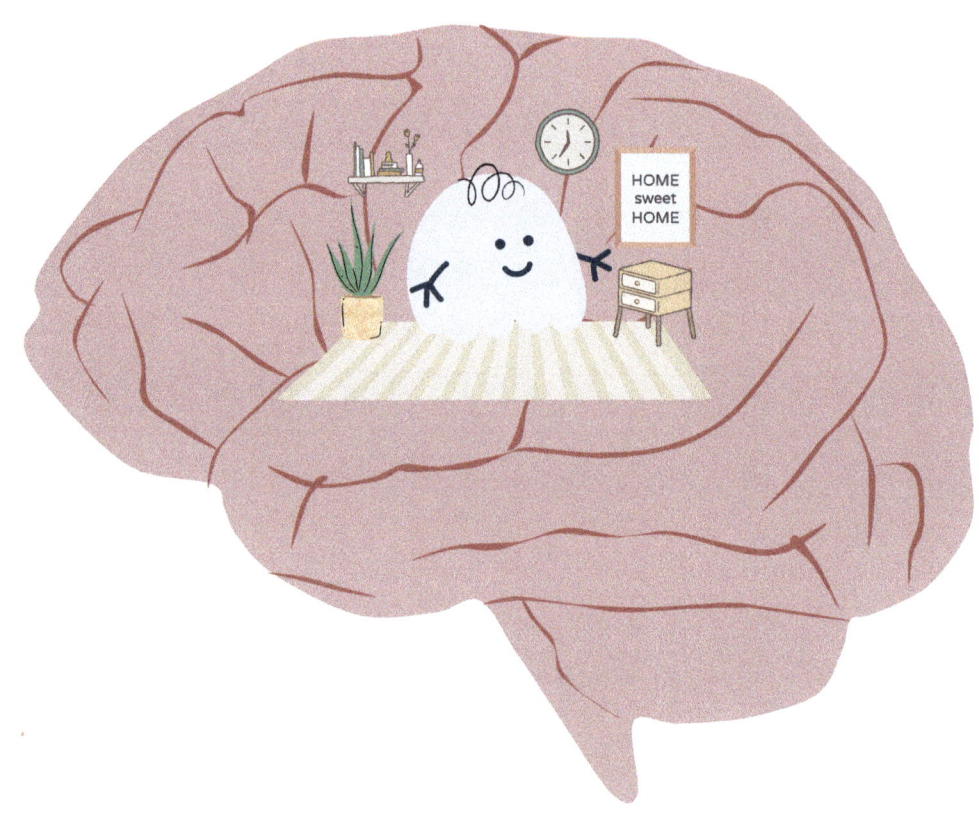

I can fill you up with worry and leave you feeling dread.

I'm the voice that whispers doubt in every choice you make.

The fear of failure and the unknown that never seems to shake.

I can make your palms so sweaty and your heart race super fast.

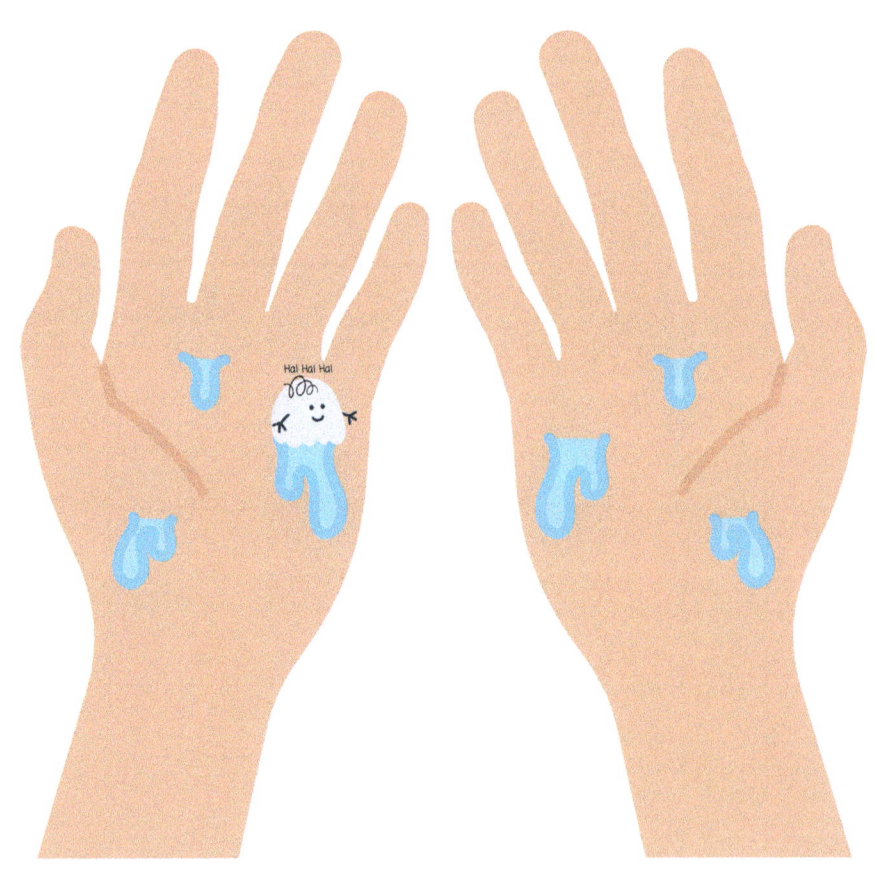

I can make it hard to catch your breath
"How long will this last?"

I'm the weight upon your shoulders that you can never seem to shake.

The nagging voice inside that tells you "You're a phoney! You're a fake!"

I can make you feel so helpless and question who you are.

I'm the constant nagging thought that you're not very going far.

But here's the thing, my dear friend you don't have to fight alone.

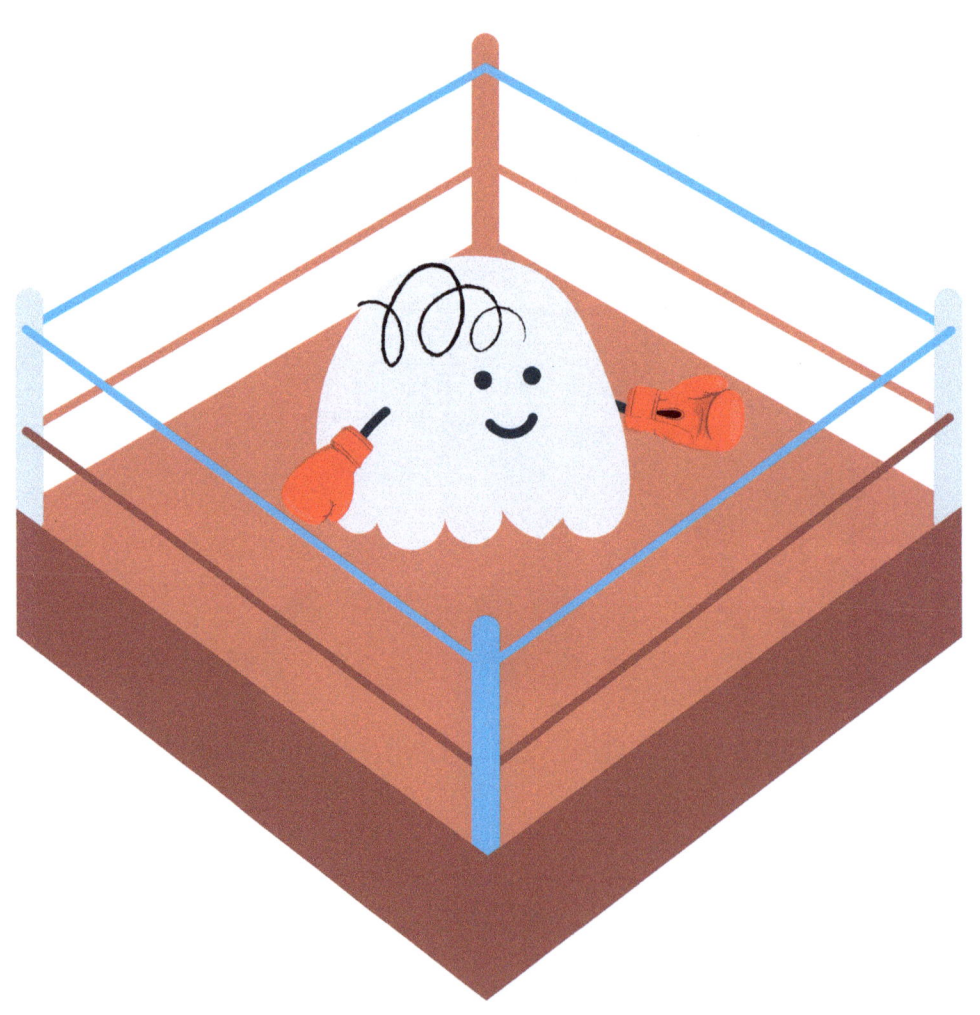

There are people who can help you and a brighter future to be shown.

Take a moment to breathe in
and let it out real slow.

For though I may be with you
you have the strength to grow.

You can talk to someone
and share what's on your mind.

They can help you face your fears
and leave the anxious thoughts behind.

You can learn new coping skills to help you when I come around.

You can challenge my voice within
and enjoy the strength you've found.

So take my hand, my dear friend
and don't let go too soon.

For though I may be with you
you don't have to stay in this cocoon.

Together we can face the world
and all that it may bring.

For though I may be anxiety
you are a powerful human being.

www.ingramcontent.com/pod-product-compliance
Lightning Source LLC
Chambersburg PA
CBHW042033100526
44587CB00029B/4401